POSITIVE THINKING

*Change Your Thinking From
Negative To Positive And Become An
Optimist For Life*

By Gerard Johnson

TABLE OF CONTENTS

Conclusion

Legal & Disclaimer

Legal & Disclaimer

Introduction

I want to thank you and congratulate you for downloading the book, *"Positive Thinking"*.

This book contains proven steps and strategies on how to master positive thinking techniques so that you can live the best possible life. If you have tried to master positive thinking techniques, and faced challenges or failed in the past, this is the book that you need. In addition to explaining why positive thinking may have failed you in the past, there is comprehensive information to help you understand how you can overcome these failures, so that you live a fully positive lifestyle.

As you start your journey into lasting positive energy, you will find the tools to help you conquer and overcome negative energy, so that it no longer secretly holds you back. It will also be easier to develop a positive attitude as you learn the necessary lessons to help you see the good in all situations.

Never again will you face any scenario that brings you down or robs your joy. This book has everything that you need to turn challenges into adventures, and negativity into positivity. Find out how you can use positive energy to come up with a plan of action that will make life worth living.

Thanks again for downloading this book, I hope you enjoy it!

Chapter 1

Making Positivity Your Focus

Consider a glass that is empty on a table, next to a jug of water. You pour water in to the glass until it is reaches the halfway level. How would you describe the glass – is it half empty, or half full? This is an age old test that is able to let you know whether you are an optimist or a pessimist. Seeing the glass has half empty means you are pessimistic with a negative outlook on life, yet, if you see the glass as half full, then you are an optimist with a positive mind-set. Simple, yet powerful.

Positive thinking is about being the optimist, looking for the good things in life to focus on, to ensure that you are able to benefit from the positivity that is all around you. Being positive makes you feel great. However, it is difficult to be positive all the time, as there are so many opportunities to experience negativity in daily life. Therefore, positive thinking requires your conscious effort.

A Day in Negativity

Imagine that you wake up in the morning in a great mood. The sun is shining, you are on schedule and everything looks set to be fantastic. You put on the radio to find out what is happening with the traffic and you hear a breaking news bulletin – fifteen people have been involved in a serious car crash. Suddenly, you no longer feel so positive. You make it to work on time, and just as your mood begins to lift again, you get called into your boss's office. There is a client that is not happy about your work and has demanded that it be redone. You begin to doubt your abilities and your positive mood takes a nose dive again.

While you struggle to redo the client's work, you find that you become easily annoyed with your co-workers, and your bad mood means that they all keep away from you or respond in kind. What started off as a fabulous day has now completely been filled with negativity.

The interesting fact about this entire scenario is that you had the power to change every single negative occurrence, by focusing on positive thinking. While it may not appear that you were actively thinking negative thoughts or attracting negativity, the mistake at hand was that you were not actively thinking positive thoughts, to ensure that the negative thoughts do not have the room to take root.

Here is how you could have done things differently. At the beginning of the day, you should not have put on the radio to find out what was happening with the traffic. Instead, you should have applied positive thinking and expected the traffic to be flowing smoothly while on your way to work. At work, when you were called into your boss's office, instead of allowing the clients criticism to affect your self-esteem, you should accept that you may not be on the same page, and find out exactly what was wrong so that you can correct that component. With your co-workers, remaining cheerful and friendly no matter what you may be facing can completely transform your atmosphere at work. Positivity always reflects back to you.

All it takes is looking at situations from a positive perspective, and it becomes possible to stand out amongst all the negatives. This is one of the secrets to positive thinking.

Why is Positivity Important?

It is always possible to live a life that is better than the one you have now. Think about it. There must be some area in your life that you believe needs to be improved on, or that can be transformed so that you experience joy and fulfillment. The easiest way of carrying out that transformation is with positive thinking. Positive thinking embodies various attributes including being able to make positive affirmations, filling the mind with positive thoughts, being optimistic, and quietening the voice within you that speaks negativity. The next chapter will teach you the best way that you can develop your positivity.

Chapter 2

Developing your Positivity

Lighting a candle requires a match. When the match is struck, it gives off a small spark which then becomes a flame, and this flame is used to light the wick of the candle, otherwise it will go out. The candle wick then radiates light much further that what the match was able to accomplish, meaning, that it gives off more energy.

Positivity is similar to this, as it always starts off as something small within you, and the more positive you are, the more your radiate positivity and give out positive energy. There are three different ways that you can get positive energy. You could develop it, transform your anxiety into positivity or attract it into your life. Here is how you can explore these ways.

Developing Positive Energy

What you are thinking on the inside, guides the actions that you have on the outside. If you want to develop positive energy, you must begin with positive thoughts. However, how can you be sure that you have developed these positive thoughts? You must use your feelings as a guide.

When you are feeling good, happy and free, you have positive energy around you. This energy will encourage you to react in a positive way to any situation, such that, anyone interacting with you will directly benefit from your good mood. Positive energy calls for you to be present, and to consciously carry out actions that keep you positive.

Developing positive energy requires you to quieten your mind, and naturally carry out actions or exercise that energize you and make you feel good. You cannot expect to generate positive energy from drugs or other artificial treatments. These temporary 'feel good' items will elevate your mood, however, they are not sustainable and once the effects have worn off, you will likely feel worse than when you started off. Instead, you can develop positive energy in the following ways: -

- Listening to amazing music that gets you dancing.

- Clearing your mind with creative writing in a journal or a book.

- Meditation and Yoga

- Finding reasons to be grateful for every moment in your life

These simple methods ensure that you take away focus from negative energy, immediately diminishing its power, and instead, focus on positive energy which brings you to the present and ensures that you can take advantage of the incredible power of positivity.

Transforming Anxiety into Positive Energy

Perhaps the greatest barrier to our positive energy is anxiety that leads to attracting negative energy. Controlling your anxiety is simple, even when it seems that the anxiety may overwhelm you. It is necessary that you determine the root cause of your anxiety so that you can control it. When you do this, you will find it possible to determine how you choose to feel about a situation, and how you really feel about it. If you have a phobia for spiders, you choose to feel fear, scream or run away from the spider in case something happens. How you may really feel is that they are creatures which seem disgusting and since you do not understand them, you would rather keep away from them.

The powerful vibrations that you release when you experience fear and anxiety that paralyses you can be transformed into vibrations of positive energy that liberate you. Realizing that you are in control of what you are thinking and feeling will make it easier to draw more positive energy towards you.

Take the spiders for example. If you are afraid of them, try and determine what causes your fear, and when you begin to feel anxious. Is it when you see them or think of them? By going to the root of the problem, you may find that it is not so much the spider that you are afraid of, it is the meaning of that spider that scares you. Changing this meaning into something positive will change your anxiety, this making it possible for you to have more positive energy.

Attracting Positive Energy

Positive thinking is directly linked to attracting positive energy. The thoughts that you choose to have will shape the positive energy that you attract. For the best results, here are some thoughts that you can try: -

- Start your day with positivity. When you get out of bed in the morning, make the firm decision that you will have a great day. Believe it within you, and go through the motions of the day as though your intention for a good day is guaranteed. The better you feel; the more positivity you will attract to you.

- Think about the relationships that you have in your life. How many fill you with joy and how many do not? In order to attract positive energy, you must reduce the relationships which give you emotional anxiety, and instead focus on the relationships where there is open communication, mutual respect and support, and trust.

- Take responsibility for yourself and your life. Examine where you are in life, and should you require improvement in any area, own the actions that you need to take. Register in programs, find a support group, read a book – anything that will call for action towards achieving the goal. This will help you realize that you are in control of the direction of your life, and the empowerment that comes from this will attract positive energy.

- When your mind is bringing you down with negative thoughts and making you feel as though you cannot function, look for someone that you can help. A person who has problems which are worse than yours will help you realize that your situation can be dealt with easily, which will undoubtedly make you feel better.

There is a timeless formula for positive energy which is: Feeling Good = Positive Energy.

Positive Energy in Your Life

Have you ever walked past a person and felt a shiver rush up your spine? You cannot explain what you feel coherently, though you do know that you want to get as far away from that person as possible. This is the effect of negative energy in a person's life. Even without you opening your mouth and saying something, there will be something about you that radiates negativity. You do not want to be this type of person.

To radiate positivity so that it is a part of your life which reflects to everyone around you, do not dwell on negative situations. The more you think negative thoughts, the darker your mood becomes. Realize that there as things that are beyond your control, and trust that your higher being or the universe will show you the right way to deal with them. Do not talk about them as this simply ensures that they have more energy and command in your life.

Therefore, when you have a disease that is making you feel terrible, do not talk about the disease. Talk about the healing that you are receiving from taking care of yourself.

A problem at work should not be your discussion over a glass of wine at the end of the evening. Instead, a discussion on looking for a better job or improving your learning for a promotion should be the focus. By changing your words, you are ensuring that negativity cannot take a hold of you.

For a positive life, let go of the things that you have been holding on to from the past, and learn to say no when you mean no, so that you do not feel powerless. In addition, learn to adopt an attitude of gratitude and you will see positivity show up in your life. Remember, you have all the power to control your actions and mood.

Chapter 3

The Power of Positive Thinking

Having everything that you have always wanted is possible if you make use of the power of positive thinking. If you were to ask the most successful people in the world to tell you the secrets of their success, the one factor that they will have in common is that they have a healthy mental attitude, never give up, and believe that they are going to make it. This is positive thinking in action.

Positive thinking enables you to become focused on your goals, which changes your attitude and approach towards the steps that you take to bring these goals to life. You will find that in your life, things seem to work out for your benefit, without significant effort. This is governed by a key law. The law of attraction.

The Law of Attraction

The law of attraction states that like attracts like. It also shows that you have control of every situation in your life, both good and bad, because of the thoughts that are happening within your mind. Therefore, if you are stuck in traffic and are late for a meeting, it is your thoughts that contributed to that situation. If you suffer from a bad breakup where you are betrayed or disrespected, it is your thoughts that caused these circumstances. If you run by a lucky period where everything seems to be going your way, this is a result of your thoughts.

As good things happen in your life, you will gladly accept that your mind is in total control of these thoughts and circumstances, yet, when what is happening is not so great, you feel as though everything is out of your control. This is not the case as you are in control of everything, both good and bad. It is all in your mind.

With the law of attraction, your thoughts will manifest as physical things and occurrences in your life. Having this in mind, it is essential that you have positive thoughts, in every circumstance that you may be facing in order to attract positive energy and positive results. This can easily be called 'looking at the brighter side of life.'

Here is a living example. You get to your workplace only to find that there has been an awful accident and fire has destroyed all of your computers and paper files. The projects that you have been working for are gone, as is information on all your clients that is vital for you to execute your job well. There is so much that needs to be done in order for you to catch up. Rather than dramatically falling to your knees, looking up and screaming why, you could look at this scenario as if it is not the end of the world.

First, be thankful that you were not at work during the fire as you may have lost your life. Second, luckily you saved all your clients phone numbers on your cell phone which is in your possession, so you have a starting point to get all your data. You also have access to your email allowing you to trace back information, and most of your data is also saved in a cloud. Since you are insured, you will get the money required to set up again, and this time, it can be better than before. Changing your thoughts to the positive will attract positive outcomes towards you, thus improving the situation you are facing.

Making Positive Thinking Work for You

There is a voice in your head that is always speaking to you, and it is this voice that causes you to question whether the decisions that you are making are right or wrong. This voice also causes you to give in to negative thinking, by convincing you that things are not going your way, the situation is worse than it appears and that you have no power. It is possible to switch this voice off by focusing on your thoughts and attitude. Here is how: -

Positive Affirmations

Positive affirmations are statements that you say to yourself, which are meant to have a positive effect on your conscious and your subconscious mind. When you make these affirmations, you are meant to be inspired, motivated and fully energized. The more you repeat a positive affirmation, the more your subconscious mind is able to visualize what you are saying which puts you in a positive frame of mind, and also governs your behavior, especially your actions and habits.

As you work towards using the power of positive thinking to your advantage, you will find that with a positive affirmation, you are better able to focus on your goal, and to transform your world from the inside out.

The way that you use positive affirmations is important if you are looking to have them work for your benefit. The best time to state your positive affirmations is at the start of each day, though, you can also choose to repeat your affirmations through the rest of the day. Whenever you experience any situation that draws you towards doubt and negativity, using a positive affirmation will turn it around. As you say your affirmation, remember to have the end goal in mind, and to be passionate about the words so that you feel them and believe in them.

Here are some affirmations that you can try out today:
-

- Every area of my life is successful.

- Happiness always seems to find me.

- Each day, my health is getting better and better.

- Money is attracted to me and flows into my life.

- My family and friends are brimming with love for me.

The more you state these affirmations and believe in them, the faster positivity is able to manifest in your daily life.

Chapter 4

Powerfully Fighting Negative Thoughts

It is possible that you are so wrapped up in your negative thinking that you find it difficult to identify a negative thought so that you can overcome it. Learning how to deal with negative thoughts is important because without this lesson, your negativity could cause you to develop a dysfunctional thinking pattern. In the worst case scenario, negative thinking could lead to mental disorders like depression, and physically, could result in the breakdown of your body systems as you lose the will to live.

To fight negative thoughts, you must know what they are, and immediately replace them with constructive positive thoughts. This needs your determination, persistence and commitment, and the end results shall be worthwhile.

Negative Thinking Patterns

Negative thinking can be identified in several main patterns which are explained as follows: -

Personalization

Some people call this playing the victim, and others refer to it as having a pity party. Either way, personalization deals with self-blame for any negative occurrence in your life, or even outside your day to day existence.

Filtration

This negative thinking pattern occurs when you are actively looking for negativity in everything, and even when there are many positives to be considered, you choose to filter them out. You see positive occurrences as a fluke, and find a way to explain why they do not count

Polarization

When you choose to polarize a situation, you see it in either black or white. This limits the way that you respond to something, as you will say it is either good or bad. You choose not to consider the various shades of grey, or explanations for the circumstances.

Catastrophizing

The next negative thinking pattern is catastrophizing where you are always expecting the worst to happen. You go into situations with the firm belief that things will not work out for you and what you are doing is a bad idea.

Overgeneralization

This happens when you believe that if one thing goes wrong, then there will be a never ending pattern of negative thinking. Everything becomes a disaster, and your entire world will come to an abrupt end.

As you read through these four negative thinking patterns, you will find that at some point in your life you have had them. Perhaps you still have

them. Negative thinking patterns will affect your ability to move forward with positivity, though now that you have identified them, you can try the following to transform them.

Negative Thinking and Your Body

Negative thoughts affect more than your mind; they also affect your body. This is because negative thoughts have been found to occur in the most primitive section of your brain. This part is known as the amygdala and it is responsible for your flight or fight response when you sense danger. It reacts quickly creative changes in your physical being. When you have negative thoughts, you may experience your muscles tightening, breathing increasing, change in blood pressure, a racing heart or a rise in your body temperature.

If you are finding it a challenge to identify your negative thoughts, even with the explanations provided in this chapter, you can watch out for your physical response.

Overcoming Negative Thinking

Before you go further, try out this exercise. Go into a quiet room with dim lighting where you know you will not be disturbed or distracted by outside noise. You will need to take a total of ten minutes in the room (you can set

a timer). Sit or lie down in the most comfortable position for you. Try to clear your mind of the thoughts of the day, while taking in deep breaths. Now, you need to be mindful, and listen to your mind instead of fighting it.

Your inner voice will begin speaking, saying all sorts of different things. Reminding you of things that you have not done, or wondering why you are doing this exercise. Allow yourself to listen to what it is saying, which is how you talk to yourself. Ask yourself, are you saying nice things that uplift you? Do you feel bad after listening to your inner voice? How are your emotions?

If you have been paying attention, you will also notice that as your thoughts become more negative, your breathing becomes faster and shallower. Now, identify which of the negative thinking patters is happening. Listen to your inner voice, and argue back with logic and reasoning. If your inner voice is telling you that you are overweight and will not amount to anything, tell it that you are eating healthier meals and are willing to be patient so that you get lasting results.

Do this for every negative thought that you have within the tem minutes. Once the timer goes off, you will feel better, more empowered and positive.

In addition, you should ask yourself whether the negative thoughts that you are having are rooted in reality, or whether they have developed due to your active imagination. Picture your friend describing to you what is happening in your own head. What advice would you give to your friend? You will find that although you have been putting yourself down, you would not like it if someone did something similar to someone that you cared about.

Turn away from the habit of negative thinking, as you are damaging your mental health as well as the relationships that you have with the people who are around you. Do not allow your mind to distort your reality.

Chapter 5

Using Positive Thinking for a Better Life

You now have some techniques at your fingertips to encourage positive thinking, meaning that through the day, you are able to redirect your thoughts so that you consistently bring your mind back to positivity. Doing this on a daily basis over a period of time can result in a better life, yet, it seems like it shall take considerable hard work and effort to guarantee results. What do you do when you find yourself slipping and unable to sustain your positivity? How can you ensure that you never allow the power of positive thinking to slip through your fingers? There are three actions that you ensure that positive thinking leads you to living a better life.

Sustain Positive Thinking

Whether you like it or not, your life will go through ups and downs. That is because so many different factors can affect your daily existence. Consider the fact that you are using the power of positive thinking to the best of your ability, but you are around someone who is vested in their negativity. It can become easy for their negativity to affect your positivity, driving you towards a bad mood. Here are seven essential steps that you can take to sustain positive thinking, no matter what the circumstances may be.

Step 1: You ARE in Control

You are in complete control of your reality, and the way that you deal with things in the world. Therefore, you can make the choice on how to react to an experience, whether it is positive or negative. You can choose to see the bright side of every situation.

Step 2: Exercise is Excellent

When you exercise, feel good chemicals are released into your blood stream, and the course through your body up until your brain. This is an easy way to get into a good mood. To remain positive for an extended period, take time to exercise in the morning before you start your activities for the day, as well as in the evening, just after you have completed work. Listening to your favorite music as you exercise will also help sustain your elevated mood.

Step 3: The Power in Your Words

How was your day? Fine. This question and answer seem quite basic, yet, by changing the way you respond, it becomes possible to sustain a positive thought. Instead of using words like 'fine' or 'ok', use words with power like fantastic, fabulous, or great. These words have a powerful effect on your positivity, and can also affect the person you are interacting with.

Step 4: Listen to Positive Messages

Find audio books, movies, and videos that are all about positivity. If there is someone that you admire for their accomplishments, a mentor or someone who simply inspires you, listen to their story. This will motivate you and help you feel good about yourself and your path in life. By learning about the steps that they have taken to attract positivity, you can emulate their actions. The great thing about doing this is that you are not restricted by time or activity, whenever and wherever it is convenient for you, you can listen to these messages.

Step 5: An Attitude of Gratitude

Keep track of all the great things that happen to you on a daily basis. Call this journal your gratitude journal. You need to be grateful for the big things as well as the little things in life. Little things are those that you experience each day without giving much thought, such as having food to eat for every meal. Big things include a promotion at work that you have been hoping for.

Step 6: Stimulate Your Attitude

To sustain a positive attitude, you need to figure out ways that you can stimulate your attitude. This will call for you to try out different activities that encourage you to feel great more often. This may seem as though you are living your best life, or being young at heart. Even when you do not feel well, have lost interest in what is happening around you, or have lost some of your confidence, shifting your attitude with positive acts will increase the positivity in your life.

Step 7: Look into the Future

Link your positivity to a goal that you want to attain in the future, rather than one that you want to attain in the present moment. This will make it easier for you to commit to positivity, rather than using positivity for immediate gain. If you are thinking positive thoughts to attract a parking space when you are at the mall, you should refocus that energy on thinking positive thoughts to purchase a better car. You will find that the positive thoughts you send out are considerably more powerful.

Chapter 6

12 Positive Thinking Habits

You have the power to grow your positive thinking by adopting simple habits. A habit is something that you do repeatedly until it becomes a part of you such that you do the actions automatically. Being able to think positively without effort will make it easier for you to live your life in an unending cycle of positivity. This means that you will have what you want, when you want, enjoy happiness and success, all while having your positive attitude affect those around you. Here are thirty fail-free habits that you can incorporate into your daily life.

1. ***Make Each Challenge an Adventure*** – Every time that you are faced with a challenge, stop yourself from believing that it is a dead-end and there is no resolution. Instead, accept that there are some things that will happen out of your control, and see each challenge as an adventure where you can

win at the end, or learn a valuable lesson.

2. **Deep Breathing** – When telling people to calm down, deep breathing is often recommended. It also has the power of changing the way that you feel, transforming a negative thought into a positive one. Use deep breathing whenever you find yourself slipping out of positivity and you will find that your mood becomes balanced once again.

3. **Spread Your Love** – Sharing love is an excellent way of attracting positive energy, and keeping it. You can do this by simple sharing a smile. This in turn will make other people smile as well, which quickly spreads a feeling of happiness. It is amazing how such a small action can have an incredible impact.

4. **Give Hugs** – Close physical contact with another person, especially when it is based in love or friendship, will immediately elevate your mood and move your mind towards positive thoughts. As humans, we love to

respond to touch and feel close to others due to this. We respond by giving out positive energy, especially when on the receiving end.

5. ***Change the Word 'have' with 'get'*** – Doing this will ensure that you experience gratitude and positivity at the highest levels. Instead of saying, 'I have to pay my bills' or 'I have go out shopping' say the words, 'I get to pay my bills' or 'I get to go out shopping'. These are words that change your attitude and increase the positivity you feel within you.

6. ***Stop saying 'always' and 'never'*** – Here are another two words that are easy to say, and both have negative energy. Stating them is absolute in nature, and condemns a person or a situation. Telling a colleague 'you never communicate' or a spouse 'you are always late' often makes a simple situation worse than it is, because it is unlikely that the never or always are based on truth. If you do use these words, make sure you only use them in a positive affirmation.

7. **Pick your Battles** – When surrounded by negative people, it is easy to get sucked into their negativity. Teach yourself how to say no when faced with a situation where others are complaining. When you choose not to validate or entertain complaints, then people are less likely to complain to you.

8. **Find Hope in Tragedy** – One of the hardest times to use positive thinking is when faced with a tragedy such as a death or traumatic experience. To remain positive in these situations, think about the success stories of others who have overcome worse challenges and find hope. In a short period, you will no longer experience anxiety or devastation.

9. **Accept Rejection** – No matter how hard you try, you cannot please everyone. Therefore, you will go through times when you are rejected, whether it is in personal relationships, the workplace or society at large. Do not give rejection the power to delve you into negative thinking. Instead, accept

rejection and always look for the opportunity that comes from it.

10. ***Be Solution Oriented*** – You will face problems at some point even when you have positive energy all the time. To remain with positive energy, you should think about the solutions to the problems, rather than the devastation of the problems. You will find that with time, you are always able to make things better.

11. ***Stay Present*** – Once you are facing an issue, make sure that you focus on the problem in the present, instead of using your energy thinking about the problem in the future, or bringing up incidences from the past. Losing focus makes it difficult to remain positive, and also brings up conflicting emotions that feed negativity. By being present, you can find a positive solution to a specific problem.

12. ***Put Yourself First*** – Positive thinking extends beyond your mind and

also affect you physically and mentally. In order to habitually think positively, you must take care of your body and your mind. This means that you stay in shape, get rest when it is necessary, and live a healthy lifestyle. These actions ensure that you live without experiencing stress or anxiety.

Conclusion

Thank you again for downloading this book!

I hope this book was able to help you to find a quick and simple solution to positive thinking. At this point, you will have mastered several key techniques as follows: -

- How to create your own positive energy through harboring positive thoughts.

- Why it is essential for you to make positivity your focus, when looking to accomplish the best in life.

- The reason that negative thoughts have controlled you, and what you can do to change this immediately.

- The tools that you need to sustain positive thinking for the rest of your life.

- Habits of positive people that will keep you in check.

The next step is to live your life through positive thoughts, so that you can have positive scenarios manifest before you. With this comprehensive book, you will find that positive thinking, which may once have been elusive, becomes a way of life. You can trust that your life will never be the same again, and that you are about to enter a new phase of happiness and prosperity.